Editor
Gisela Lee

Editorial Manager
Karen J. Goldfluss, M.S. Ed.

Editor-in-Chief
Sharon Coan, M.S. Ed.

Cover Artist
Jessica Orlando

Art Coordinator
Denice Adorno

Creative Director
Elayne Roberts

Imaging
James Edward Grace

Product Manager
Phil Garcia

Publisher
Mary D. Smith, M.S. Ed.

How Divide

Grades 4–6

Author

Robert Smith

Teacher Created Resources, Inc.
6421 Industry Way
Westminster, CA 92683
www.teachercreated.com

ISBN: 978-1-57690-947-8

©2000 Teacher Created Resources, Inc.
Reprinted, 2007
Made in U.S.A.

Teacher Created Resources

Table of Contents

A Note to Teachers and Parents

Welcome to the "How to" math series! You have chosen one of over two dozen books designed to give your children the information and practice they need to acquire important concepts in specific areas of math. The goal of the "How to" math books is to give children an extra boost as they work toward mastery of the math skills established by the National Council of Teachers of Mathematics (NCTM) and outlined in grade-level scope and sequence guidelines.

The design of this book is intended to allow it to be used by teachers or parents for a variety of purposes and needs. Each of the units contains one or more "How to" pages and two or more practice pages. The "How to" section of each unit precedes the practice pages and provides needed information such as a concept or math rule review, important terms and formulas to remember, and/or step-by-step guidelines necessary for using the practice pages. While most "How to" pages are written for direct use by the children, in some lower-grade-level books these pages are presented as instructional pages or direct lessons to be used by a teacher or parent prior to introducing the practice pages.

About This Book

How to Divide: Grades 4–6 is intended to be used by teachers or parents for a variety of purposes and needs. Because it presents a comprehensive overview of division of whole numbers and because there are clear, simple, and readable instruction pages for each unit, the book may be used as an instruction vehicle for teaching division to students who have some initial background in the concept and familiarity with their basic multiplication/division facts.

This book can be used in whole-class directed-teaching lessons with the teacher or parent going page by page through the book. The book also lends itself to be used by a small group doing remedial work on division or individuals and small groups in earlier grades engaged in enrichment or advanced work. A teacher may want to have two tracks within her class with one moving at a faster pace and the other at a gradual pace appropriate to the ability or background of her students.

Teachers and parents working with children who are relatively new to the concept or who don't know their basic facts fluently should insist that children use a times tables chart until students learn the tables through time and use. Students should also be allowed to use the calculator to check the accuracy of their work. This reduces the need for teacher correction and allows the material to be self-corrected if that works with your students. (Remainders on the calculator will be expressed in decimal format, but the whole number answers will be the same. Students can also use the calculator for checking division by multiplying the quotient times the divisor and adding the remainder.)

Where possible, teachers should integrate the opposite operation and help students recognize that multiplication and division are inverse operations closely related in both concept and process. The multiplication book in this series is done along the same lines and complements this integration.

If students get stuck on a specific concept or unit within this book, review the material and allow students to redo the pages which were giving them difficulty. Don't accelerate the process or skip much of the material in the book. It is preferable that children find the work easy and gradually advance to the more difficult concepts as the book is designed.

This book is designed to match the suggestions of the National Council of Teachers of Mathematics. They strongly support the learning of division and other processes in the context of problem solving and real-world applications. Use every opportunity to have students apply these new skills in classroom situations and at home. This will reinforce the value of the skill as well as the process.

This book matches a number of NCTM standards, including these main topics and specific features:

Computation and Estimation

How to Divide: Grades 4–6 highlights the use of various mental math activities and emphasizes the development of proficiency in division calculations. Students use estimation to determine the reasonableness of an answer. A wide variety of instructional models and explanations for the gradual and thorough development of division concepts and processes are provided. Specific techniques for dealing with word applications are highlighted and integrated through the text. Students are encouraged to select the appropriate tool for computing specific types of division problems from among mental arithmetic, pencil and paper, and calculator methods. Calculator usage is integrated within the text.

Mathematical Connections

The problems in this book help students see how mathematical ideas are related, especially in terms of division and its inverse operation, multiplication. They also see the connections with percentages, averages, square roots, and other math concepts. Students recognize the use and application of division in mathematics and in their daily lives.

Mathematics as Problem Solving

This book offers opportunities to apply basic division computational skills in word-problem formats and with real-life applications. Students will also develop facility and confidence in their computational ability and their ability to apply mathematics meaningfully.

Numbers and Number Relationships

The material in this book conforms well to this standard which emphasizes the need to understand, represent, and apply numbers in equivalent forms such as decimals, percentages, and square roots.

Mathematical Connections

The problems in this book help students see how mathematical ideas are related. The connections to other disciplines and to the world at large are also stressed.

Other Standards

This book also focuses on learning computational skills like division within the context of other math concepts such as patterns, functions, and sequences.

Facts to Know

Long division is the process used to do harder division problems. Use this Division Code to help you learn the process.

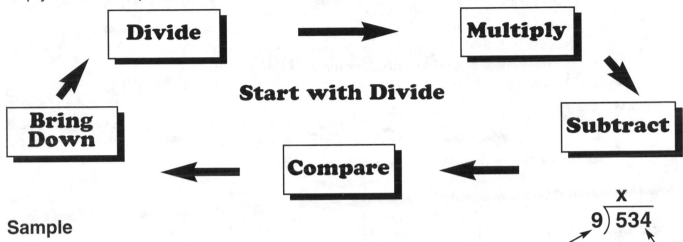

Start with Divide

Sample

Using the Division Code above, do this sample problem step by step.

$$9\overline{)534} \quad \text{divisor} \quad \text{dividend}$$

Divide
1. Begin division with the number in the dividend closest to the divisor (9). The number 5 is not divisible by 9 so place an X over the 5.

$$\overset{X}{9\overline{)534}}$$

Multiply
2. The number 53 is divisible by 9 because 9 x 5 = 45 is the closest multiple of 9 to the dividend 53. Place 5 in the quotient. Write the number 45 under the number 53.

$$\overset{X5}{9\overline{)534}} \\ 45$$

Subtract
3. Subtract 45 from 53. The difference (or remainder) is 8.

$$\overset{X5}{9\overline{)534}} \\ -45 \\ 8$$

Compare
4. Is the remainder less than the divisor? In this problem the remainder 8 is less than the divisor 9.

Bring Down
5. Bring down the number 4 next to the number 8.

$$\overset{X5}{9\overline{)534}} \\ -45\downarrow \\ 84$$

Start Over
6. Divide 84 into 9.

7. Multiply 9 x 9. The product is 81. Place 9 in the quotient and the number 81 under the number 84.

8. Subtract 81 from 84 and the difference is 3. This is the remainder. It is "left over" since it cannot be divided by 9 to produce a whole number. Since there are no more digits to bring down, write R3 to show it as the remainder. The answer (or quotient) for this problem is 59 R3.

$$\overset{X59\ R3}{9\overline{)534}} \\ -45\downarrow \\ 84 \\ -81 \\ \text{remainder} \rightarrow 3$$

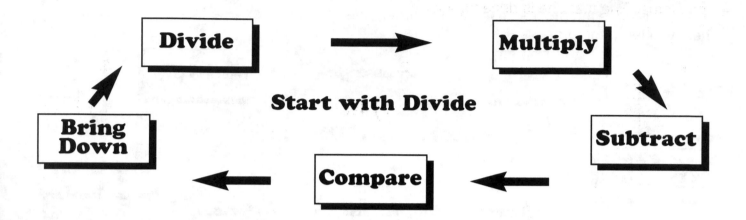

Divide → **Multiply**

Start with Divide

Bring Down **Subtract**

Compare

Directions: Using the information on page 5 and the Division Code above, solve the division problems below.

1. 7)78   2. 5)84   3. 2)26   4. 6)67   5. 3)86

6. 4)99   7. 9)81   8. 1)34   9. 6)78   10. 9)96

11. 5)56   12. 4)57   13. 2)33   14. 3)56   15. 8)90

16. 4)67   17. 1)23   18. 7)46   19. 5)44   20. 6)56

21. 9)90   22. 7)35   23. 3)38   24. 4)87   25. 2)47

1 Practice • • • • • • • • • • Using One-Digit Divisors with Three-Digit Dividends

Directions: Use the information on page 5 and the Division Code to help you do these problems. The first one is done for you.

1.

```
   x91
5) 455
  - 45
     5
   - 5
     0
```

2. 7) 498

3. 6) 372

4. 7) 437

5. 5) 266

6. 8) 416

7. 9) 487

8. 8) 638

9. 7) 439

10. 4) 303

11. 4) 398

12. 8) 456

Follow the steps in the sample problem below to solve long division with four-digit dividends.

Sample

1. Because the digit nearest the divisor (6) could not be divided by 7, place an X over the 6. Then divide 63 by 7. The answer is 9. Place 9 in the quotient.

2. Subtract 63 – 63. The answer is 0. Next, bring down the 8 and divide by 7.

3. Multiply 7 x 1 = 7 and then subtract 8 – 7. The answer is 1. Place 1 in the quotient. Bring down the 7 next to the 1.

4. Divide 17 by 7. After multiplying 7 x 2 = 14, which is the closest multiple of 7 to 17, place 2 in the quotient. Subtract 17 – 14. The answer is 3 (or the remainder for the problem).

5. The final answer is 912 R3.

$$
\begin{array}{r}
\text{x 912 R3} \\
7\overline{)6{,}387} \\
-\ 63\downarrow\ \ \\
\hline
8\ \ \\
-\ 7\downarrow \\
\hline
17 \\
-\ 14 \\
\hline
3
\end{array}
$$

Directions: Use the information above and on page 5 and the Division Code to help you do these problems.

1.

$$8\overline{)4897}\quad R\_\_$$

2.

$$8\overline{)5529}\quad R\_\_$$

3.

$$6\overline{)2248}\quad R\_\_$$

4.

$$9\overline{)3756}\quad R\_\_$$

5.

$$7\overline{)6213}\quad R\_\_$$

6.

$$6\overline{)2935}\quad R\_\_$$

7.

$$5\overline{)5629}\quad R\_\_$$

8.

$$4\overline{)5821}\quad R\_\_$$

9.

$$9\overline{)9813}\quad R\_\_$$

Facts to Know

In division there is a set of rules that makes division easier because of a pattern which indicates that a certain dividend is divisible by a specific divisor.

Rules of Divisibility

Divisor	Rule: A number is divisible by _____ if . . .
2	the last digit of the dividend (or ones digit) is 0, 2, 4, 6, or 8. (**Example**—126 ÷ 2 = 63)
3	the sum of the digits in a dividend is divisible by 3. (**Example**—126: 1 + 2 + 6 = 9; 9 is divisible by 3 so 126 is divisible by 3)
4	the number formed by the last two digits of the dividend is divisible by 4. (**Example**—428: the last two digits are 28; 28 is divisible by 4 so 428 is divisible by 4)
5	the last digit of the dividend is 0 or 5. (**Example**—115 is divisible by 5, but 412 is not divisible by 5)
6	the dividend is divisible by 2 and 3. (**Example**—642: the ones digit is even so it is divisible by 2, and the sum of the digits 6 + 4 + 2 = 12 is divisible by 3 so 642 is divisible by 6)
9	the sum of the digits in the dividend is divisible by 9. (**Example**—693: the sum of the digits 6 + 9 + 3 is 18; 18 is divisible by 9 so 693 is divisible by 9)
10	the last digit of the dividend (or ones digit) is 0. (**Example**—250: the last digit of the number is 0 so 250 is divisible by 10)

Directions: Use the Rules of Divisibility on page 9 to solve the problems on this page. The first one has been done for you.

1.

$$
\begin{array}{r}
381 \\
2\overline{)\,762} \\
-6 \\
\hline
16 \\
-16 \\
\hline
2 \\
-2 \\
\hline
0
\end{array}
$$

2.

$5\overline{)\,465}$

3.

$3\overline{)\,372}$

4.

$4\overline{)\,164}$

5.

$2\overline{)\,286}$

6.

$5\overline{)\,675}$

7.

$3\overline{)\,672}$

8.

$4\overline{)\,352}$

9.

$5\overline{)\,870}$

10.

$2\overline{)\,450}$

11.

$3\overline{)\,8901}$

12.

$4\overline{)\,5680}$

13.

$2\overline{)\,7912}$

14.

$5\overline{)\,5230}$

15.

$3\overline{)\,9807}$

16.

$2\overline{)\,2368}$

10

Directions: Use the Rules of Divisibility on page 9 to solve the problems on this page. The first one has been done for you.

1.
```
        x91
    9) 819
     - 81
    ───────
         9
    -    9
    ───────
         0
```

2.
```
  6) 324
```

3.
```
  9) 765
```

4.
```
  10) 790
```

5.
```
  9) 558
```

6.
```
  6) 336
```

7.
```
  10) 450
```

8.
```
  6) 642
```

9.
```
  9) 279
```

10.
```
  10) 670
```

11.
```
  10) 7430
```

12.
```
  6) 3462
```

13.
```
  9) 9819
```

14.
```
  10) 5610
```

15.
```
  9) 3321
```

16.
```
  6) 8424
```

2 Practice • • • • • • • • • • Using the Rules of Divisibility

Directions: Use the Rules of Divisibility on page 9 to solve the problems on this page.

1. $9\overline{)2142}$

2. $3\overline{)2112}$

3. $2\overline{)1998}$

4. $5\overline{)8020}$

5. $4\overline{)9248}$

6. $10\overline{)4790}$

7. $6\overline{)1272}$

8. $3\overline{)5223}$

9. $9\overline{)6327}$

10. $2\overline{)3428}$

11. $5\overline{)9905}$

12. $10\overline{)1910}$

Facts to Know

Solve every division problem step by step using the Division Code. Here is a sample problem to use as a guide or reference.

Step by Step

Divide

$$\overset{\text{X}}{20\overline{)964}}$$

1. The first number of the dividend 9 is not divisible by 20 so place an X over the 9.

2. The number 96 is divisible by 20. The closest multiple of 20 to 96 is 20 x 4 = 80. Place 4 in the quotient.

$$\begin{array}{r} \text{x4} \\ 20\overline{)964} \\ 80 \end{array}$$

Multiply

3. Multiply 20 x 4 and write the number 80 under 96.

Subtract

4. Subtract 80 from 96. The difference (or remainder) is 16.

$$\begin{array}{r} \text{x4} \\ 20\overline{)964} \\ -\underline{80} \\ 16 \end{array}$$

Compare

5. Is the remainder less than the divisor? In this problem the remainder 16 is less than the divisor 20.

Bring Down

6. Bring down the number 4 next to the number 16.

$$\begin{array}{r} \text{x4} \\ 20\overline{)964} \\ -\underline{80\downarrow} \\ 164 \end{array}$$

Start Over

7. Divide 164 by 20. You know that 20 x 8 = 160 is the closest multiple of 20 to 164. Place 8 in the quotient.

8. Multiply 8 x 20. Write the answer 160 below the number 164.

$$\begin{array}{r} \text{x48 R4} \\ 20\overline{)964} \\ -\underline{80\downarrow} \\ 164 \\ -\underline{160} \\ 4 \end{array}$$

9. Subtract 160 from 164 and the answer is 4, which is the remainder since 4 is less than the divisor 20. The answer is 48 R4.

---

3 Practice •••••••••• Dividing by 10, 100, and 1,000

When dividing by 10, 100, or 1,000, remember the following rules:

- Any number ending in zero is divisible by 10.
- Drop the zero from the dividend and you have the quotient.
- Any number ending in two zeros is divisible by 100.
- Any number ending in three zeros is divisible by 1,000.

$$10\overline{)340} = 34 \qquad 100\overline{)2,700} = 27 \qquad 1,000\overline{)498,000} = 498$$

Directions: Use the information on this page to help you practice mental math. Use paper and pencil or a calculator to check your answers.

1. $10\overline{)370}$

2. $10\overline{)570}$

3. $10\overline{)660}$

4. $10\overline{)4560}$

5. $10\overline{)7430}$

6. $100\overline{)7600}$

7. $100\overline{)6700}$

8. $100\overline{)5400}$

9. $100\overline{)7700}$

10. $100\overline{)2300}$

11. $1000\overline{)998,000}$

12. $1000\overline{)447,000}$

13. $1000\overline{)168,000}$

14. $1000\overline{)345,000}$

15. $1000\overline{)678,000}$

Directions: Use the information on page 13 to help you do these problems. The first one is done for you.

1.

```
         x23
  20) 460
    − 40
      60
    − 60
       0
```

2.

```
  30) 660
```

3.

```
  40) 840
```

4.

```
  30) 966
```

5.

```
  40) 489
```

6.

```
  20) 687
```

7.

```
  20) 849
```

8.

```
  20) 956
```

9.

```
  30) 729
```

10.

```
  50) 7500
```

11.

```
  30) 6330
```

12.

```
  20) 8860
```

13.

```
  30) 6960
```

14.

```
  20) 6420
```

15.

```
  30) 6990
```

16.

```
  60) 9667
```

3 Practice • • • • • More Division with Multiples of 10

Directions: Use the information on page 13 to help you do these problems.

1. $20\overline{)3460}$

2. $10\overline{)9030}$

3. $30\overline{)2070}$

4. $20\overline{)4000}$

5. $50\overline{)7500}$

6. $10\overline{)4860}$

7. $70\overline{)3570}$

8. $20\overline{)2680}$

9. $30\overline{)2490}$

10. $80\overline{)6480}$

11. $70\overline{)5250}$

12. $50\overline{)3100}$

Facts to Know

Use the Division Code to solve long division problems. Follow the steps in the sample problem below as a guide when doing long division problems.

Step by Step

Divide

$$\overset{\text{X}}{22\overline{)694}}$$

1. Begin division with the number in the dividend closest to the divisor (22). The number 6 is not divisible by 22 so place an X over the 6.

2. The number 69 is divisible by 22. The closest multiple of 22 to 69 is 22 x 3 = 66. Place 3 in the quotient.

$$\begin{array}{r} \text{x3} \\ 22\overline{)694} \\ -\ 66 \\ \hline 3 \end{array}$$

Multiply

3. Multiply 22 x 3 and write the number 66 under the number 69.

Subtract

4. Subtract 66 from 69. The difference (or remainder) is 3.

$$\begin{array}{r} \text{x3} \\ 22\overline{)694} \\ -\ 66\downarrow \\ \hline 34 \end{array}$$

Compare

5. Is the remainder less than the divisor? In this problem the remainder 3 is less than the divisor 22.

Bring Down

6. Bring down the number 4 next to the number 3.

$$\begin{array}{r} \text{x31} \\ 22\overline{)694} \\ -\ 66\downarrow \\ \hline 34 \\ -\ 22 \\ \hline 12 \end{array}$$

Start Over

7. Divide 34 by 22. You know that 22 x 1 = 22 is the closest multiple of 22 to 34. Place 1 in the quotient.

8. Multiply 1 x 22. Write the answer 22 below the number 34.

9. Subtract 22 from 34 and the answer is 12, which is the remainder since 12 is less than the divisor 22. The final answer is 31 R12.

$$\begin{array}{r} \text{x31 R12} \\ 22\overline{)694} \\ -\ 66\downarrow \\ \hline 34 \\ -\ 22 \\ \hline 12 \end{array}$$

Follow these steps when solving long division problems.

Sample

1. Because the first digit (6) in the dividend cannot be divided by 12, divide 66 by 12. The closest multiple of 12 to 66 is 12 x 5 = 60. Place 5 in the quotient.
2. Multiply 12 x 5 and write the number 60 below 66.
3. Subtract 60 from 66. The answer is 6.
4. Because the number 6 is less than the divisor 12, bring down the 0 and divide 60 by 12.
5. Multiply 12 x 5. The answer is 60. Place 5 in the qoutient.
6. Subtract 60 from 60. The final answer is 55.

$$
\begin{array}{r}
\mathbf{55} \\
12\overline{)660} \\
-\ 60\downarrow \\
\hline
60 \\
-\ 60 \\
\hline
0
\end{array}
$$

Directions: Use the information on page 17 and the sample above to help you do these problems. The first one is done for you.

1.
$$
\begin{array}{r}
\mathbf{21}\ R17 \\
22\overline{)479} \\
-\ 44 \\
\hline
39 \\
-\ 22 \\
\hline
17
\end{array}
$$

2. $31\overline{)975}$

3. $23\overline{)748}$

4. $21\overline{)661}$

5. $33\overline{)497}$

6. $41\overline{)453}$

7. $21\overline{)887}$

8. $33\overline{)715}$

9. $22\overline{)519}$

10. $31\overline{)428}$

11. $24\overline{)534}$

12. $22\overline{)721}$

4 Practice •••• Dividing with Two-Digit Divisors and Three-Digit Dividends

Directions: Use the information on page 17 and the Division Code to help you do these problems. The first one is done for you.

1.
```
      x23 R10
29 ) 677
    - 58
      97
    - 87
      10
```

2. 28) 754

3. 39) 828

4. 37) 443

5. 18) 628

6. 27) 634

7. 17) 420

8. 36) 843

9. 19) 431

10. 29) 909

11. 47) 741

12. 27) 603

13. 39) 841

14. 27) 635

15. 19) 661

16. 29) 971

Follow this sample problem as a guide to help you solve the long division problems on this page.

Sample

1. Because the first digit (9) in the dividend cannot be divided by 29, divide 93 by 29. The closest multiple of 29 to 93 is 29 x 3 = 87. Place 3 in the quotient.
2. Multiply 29 x 3 and write down the number 87 below 93.
3. Subtract 87 from 93. The answer is 6.
4. Bring down the 4 and divide 64 by 29.
5. Multiply 29 x 2. The answer is 58. Place 2 in the quotient.
6. Subtract 58 from 64. The answer is 6.
7. Bring down the 7 and divide 67 by 29.
8. Multiply 29 x 2. The answer is 58. Place 2 in the quotient.
9. Subtract 58 from 67. The answer is 9 (or the remainder).
10. The final answer is 322 R9.

$$\begin{array}{r} \text{x322 R9} \\ 29\overline{)9{,}347} \\ -87 \\ \hline 64 \\ -58 \\ \hline 67 \\ -58 \\ \hline 9 \end{array}$$

Directions: Use the information on page 17 and the sample above to help you do these problems.

1.

$$28\overline{)5194}$$

2.

$$41\overline{)8836}$$

3.

$$34\overline{)8325}$$

4.

$$29\overline{)6499}$$

5.

$$27\overline{)9679}$$

6.

$$49\overline{)8945}$$

7.

$$42\overline{)8956}$$

8.

$$29\overline{)7429}$$

9.

$$24\overline{)6037}$$

Facts to Know

When solving long division problems in which placeholders are used, follow these steps in this sample.

Step by Step

1. Determine if every digit in the dividend is divisible by the divisor. In this sample problem, the first digit in the dividend (6) is not divisible by the divisor (29) so an X is placed over the number 6 in the dividend.

$$\begin{array}{r} \text{X} \\ 29\overline{)6{,}021} \end{array}$$

2. The number 60 is divisible by 29. The closest multiple of 29 to 60 is 29 x 2 = 58. Place 2 in the quotient.

$$\begin{array}{r} \text{X 2} \\ 29\overline{)6{,}021} \\ -58 \\ \hline 2 \end{array}$$

3. Multiply 29 x 2 and write the number 58 below 60.

4. Subtract 60 – 58 and the answer is 2.

$$\begin{array}{r} \text{X 20} \\ 29\overline{)6{,}021} \\ -58\downarrow \\ \hline 22 \end{array}$$

5. Bring down the next digit in the dividend (2) and place it next to the 2. Is 22 divisible by 29? No, the divisor 29 is a larger number than the number 22 so place a 0 as a placeholder over the 2 in the dividend.

6. Bring down the next digit in the dividend (1) and place it next to 22. Is 221 divisible by 29? The closest multiple of 29 to 221 is 29 x 7 = 203.

$$\begin{array}{r} \text{X 20} \\ 29\overline{)6{,}021} \\ -58\downarrow\downarrow \\ \hline 221 \end{array}$$

7. Multiply 29 x 7. Place 7 in the quotient. Write the answer 203 below 221.

8. Subtract 203 from 221 and the answer (or remainder) is 18. Because the remainder (18) is not divisible by the divisor (29), the final answer to this problem is 207 R18.

$$\begin{array}{r} \text{X 207 R18} \\ 29\overline{)6{,}021} \\ -58\downarrow\downarrow \\ \hline 221 \\ -203 \\ \hline 18 \end{array}$$

5 ▶ Practice •••••••••••••• **Using Placeholders in Long Division Problems**

Use this sample problem as a guide to how to use placeholders in long division problems.

Sample

1. Because you can't divide the first number in the dividend (8) by the divisor (9), divide 81 by 9 (*Hint:* 9 x 9 = 81). Place 9 in the quotient.

2. Place a 0 as a placeholder over the 0 in the dividend because 0 is not divisible by the divisor (9).

3. Similarly, when you bring down the next digit in the dividend (2), this also is not divisible by the divisor (9) so place another 0 as a placeholder over the last digit (2) in the dividend.

4. The final answer is 900 R2 because there is a remainder of 2, and two 0 placeholders were needed in this sample problem.

$$
\begin{array}{r}
x\ 900\ R2 \\
9\overline{)8{,}102} \\
-81\ \downarrow \\
\hline
2
\end{array}
$$

Directions: Use the information on page 21 and the sample above to help you do the problems below. Remember the placeholders.

1.

$$9\overline{)812}$$

2.

$$3\overline{)611}$$

3.

$$5\overline{)5011}$$

4.

$$5\overline{)5019}$$

5.

$$8\overline{)6403}$$

6.

$$7\overline{)4906}$$

7.

$$20\overline{)215}$$

8.

$$30\overline{)3101}$$

9.

$$20\overline{)4004}$$

10.

$$40\overline{)8102}$$

11.

$$20\overline{)6105}$$

12.

$$25\overline{)5105}$$

Division Reminders

- Do every division problem step by step, using the Division Code.
- Place an X over the first digit of the dividend if it is not divisible by the divisor.
- Place a placeholder or number over every digit in the dividend.

Directions: Use the information on page 21 to help you do the problems below. Remember to use placeholders.

1.

$20\overline{)4112}$

2.

$30\overline{)6295}$

3.

$40\overline{)4219}$

4.

$25\overline{)5249}$

5.

$25\overline{)7736}$

6.

$25\overline{)2729}$

7.

$21\overline{)4367}$

8.

$22\overline{)4598}$

9.

$23\overline{)7093}$

10.

$31\overline{)6492}$

11.

$33\overline{)6892}$

12.

$33\overline{)9814}$

Division Reminders

- Do every division problem step by step, using the Division Code.
- Place an X over the first digit of the dividend if it is not divisible by the divisor.
- Place a placeholder or number over every digit in the dividend.

Directions: Use the information on page 21 to help you do the problems below. Remember to use placeholders.

1.

$$27 \overline{)5556}$$

2.

$$23 \overline{)2322}$$

3.

$$39 \overline{)7991}$$

4.

$$45 \overline{)9391}$$

5.

$$35 \overline{)7348}$$

6.

$$23 \overline{)4829}$$

7.

$$25 \overline{)7740}$$

8.

$$66 \overline{)7259}$$

9.

$$19 \overline{)3989}$$

10.

$$17 \overline{)5269}$$

11.

$$44 \overline{)9230}$$

12.

$$36 \overline{)3635}$$

Facts to Know

Estimating Quotients

You can determine if an answer in division is reasonable by learning to estimate the answers.

Sample

1. Round the divisor to the nearest 10 or 100, depending on how many digits are in the divisor. In the sample problem, the divisor 27 rounds to 30.

2. Round the dividend to the nearest 10, 100, or 1,000 so that all of the digits, except the first one are zeros. In the sample problem, the dividend 630 rounds to 600.

3. Divide 600 by 30. The answer is 20.

4. Compare your estimate to the exact answer to determine if the exact answer is reasonable.

$$27\overline{)630}$$
$$\downarrow \qquad \downarrow$$
$$30\overline{)600} \quad 20$$

$$\begin{array}{r} \textbf{x23 R9} \\ 27\overline{)630} \\ -54\downarrow \\ \hline 90 \\ -81 \\ \hline 9 \end{array}$$

The estimate of 20 and the exact answer of 23 R9 are close so the estimated answer is reasonably close to the actual answer.

Helpful Hint: The estimate and the exact answer will usually have the same number of digits.

Check Division with Multiplication

Division and multiplication are inverse or opposite operations. You can use multiplication to check your division answer this way.

Sample

quotient
$$\begin{array}{r} \textbf{x23 R9} \\ 27\overline{)630} \leftarrow \text{dividend} \\ -54 \\ \hline 90 \\ -81 \\ \hline 9 \leftarrow \text{remainder} \end{array}$$
divisor

$$\begin{array}{r} 23 \quad \text{quotient} \\ \times 27 \quad \text{divisor} \\ \hline 161 \\ +460 \\ \hline 621 \\ +9 \quad \text{remainder} \\ \hline 630 \quad \text{dividend} \end{array}$$

1. Do the division problem.

2. Multiply the quotient times the divisor.

3. If there is a remainder, add it to the multiplication product.

4. Compare this answer to the dividend. They should be the same number (630 = 630).

You can estimate a quotient to see if your answer is reasonable by following these steps:

Sample

- Round off the divisor and the dividend.

- Divide the rounded-off numbers in your mind.

- Compare your estimate to the actual answer.

Actual

$$
\begin{array}{r}
x\ 223\ R5 \\
38\overline{)8{,}479} \\
-7\,6\downarrow \\
\hline
87 \\
-76\downarrow \\
\hline
119 \\
-114 \\
\hline
5
\end{array}
$$

Estimate

$$
\begin{array}{r}
x\ 200 \\
40\overline{)8{,}000} \\
-8\,0 \\
\hline
0
\end{array}
$$

Directions: Estimate a quotient for each problem below. Then do the division to get the exact answer. Use the information above and on page 25 to help you solve these problems. The first one is done for you.

Actual	Estimate	Actual	Estimate

1.

$$
\begin{array}{r}
x19\ R9 \\
23\overline{)446} \\
-23 \\
\hline
216 \\
-207 \\
\hline
9
\end{array}
$$

$$
\begin{array}{r}
x20 \\
20\overline{)400} \\
-40 \\
\hline
0
\end{array}
$$

4.

$$
27\overline{)939}\quad x\ \ \ \ R
$$

2.

$$
39\overline{)841}\quad x\ \ \ \ R
$$

5.

$$
41\overline{)841}\quad x\ \ \ \ R
$$

3.

$$
28\overline{)625}\quad x\ \ \ \ R
$$

6.

$$
29\overline{)6459}\quad x\ \ \ \ R
$$

You can use multiplication to check division this way:

```
                    quotient
                       ↓
               x 302 R3
divisor →  25) 7,553  ← dividend
               -7 5↓↓
                  53
                 -50
                   3  ← remainder
```

```
302    quotient
X 25   divisor
1,510
+6,040
7,550
+    3   remainder
7,553  dividend
```

Check your division by multiplying the quotient and divisor (302 x 25 = 7,550) and then adding the remainder to the product (7,550 + 3).

Directions: Use the information on page 25 and in the sample above to help you solve these problems and check the answers. The first one is started for you.

Check

1.
```
          x19 R9
    23) 446
        23
        216
        207
          9
```

2.
```
         x    R
    39) 887
```

3.
```
         x    R
    21) 765
```

Check

4.
```
         x    R
    29) 913
```

5.
```
         x    R
    33) 784
```

6.
```
         x    R
    31) 4816
```

Checking More Division Problems with Multiplication

Directions: Solve the long division problems below. Use the information on page 25 to help you solve each problem. Check your division by using multiplication for each problem.

1.

$26\overline{)7915}$

2.

$33\overline{)6934}$

3.

$16\overline{)4965}$

4.

$92\overline{)9536}$

5.

$17\overline{)1428}$

6.

$53\overline{)9352}$

7.

$88\overline{)9734}$

8.

$43\overline{)9887}$

9.

$26\overline{)5644}$

10.

$76\overline{)86,734}$

11.

$65\overline{)13,120}$

12.

$14\overline{)13,962}$

Facts to Know

Use the Division Code and estimation to solve long division problems with three-digit divisors and large dividends. Follow the steps in the sample problem below as a guide when solving division problems.

1. Round the divisor (289) to the nearest hundred (300). Next round the dividend (6,743) to the nearest thousand (7,000). Solve the estimated problem. The estimated answer is 23 R100.

$$289\overline{)6{,}743}$$

2. Now solve the actual problem and see if the estimated answer is close to the actual answer. The divisor 289 does not divide into 6 or 67 so place an X above both the 6 and 7.

$$\begin{array}{r} \text{x x23 R100} \\ 300\overline{)7{,}000} \\ -6\ 00\downarrow \\ \hline 1{,}000 \\ -\ 900 \\ \hline 100 \end{array}$$

3. Divide 674 by 289. The closest multiple to 674 is 289 x 2 = 578. Place 2 in the quotient.

4. Multiply 289 x 2. Write the 2 above the 4 in the dividend and write the answer (578) below the number 674.

$$\begin{array}{r} \text{x x2} \\ 289\overline{)6{,}743} \\ -5\ 78 \\ \hline 96 \end{array}$$

5. Subtract 578 from 674. The answer is 96.

6. Compare and see if the remainder 96 is divisible by the divisor (289). In this sample problem, the remainder is less than the divisor.

$$\begin{array}{r} \text{x x2} \\ 289\overline{)6{,}743} \\ -5\ 78\downarrow \\ \hline 963 \end{array}$$

7. Bring down the 3 next to the 96.

Start Over

8. Divide 963 by 289.

9. Multiply 289 x 3. Place the 3 in the quotient and write the answer (867) below the number 963.

$$\begin{array}{r} \text{x x23 R96} \\ 289\overline{)6\ 743} \\ -5\ 78\downarrow \\ \hline 963 \\ -\ 867 \\ \hline 96 \end{array}$$

10. Subtract 867 from 963, and the difference (or remainder) is 96.

11. The final answer for this problem is 23 R96 which is very close to the estimated answer of 23 R100.

Extension

Check your calculations on a calculator by using multiplication and addition. You will discover that when you multiply 289 x 23 and then add 96 on a calculator, the answer is 6,743.

Follow this sample problem for the steps involved with using multiplication to check long division on a calculator.

1. Enter the quotient 14 into your calculator.

2. Press the [X] (multiplication) button on your calculator.

3. Enter the divisor 467 into your calculator.

4. Press the [=] button on your calculator.

5. The answer is 2,128. Add the remainder 260 to 2,218. The answer is equivalent to the answer you would get when you worked out the long division on paper (14 R260).

```
        x x14 R260
467) 6,798
    −4 67↓
      2,128
     −1,868
        260
```

Directions: Use the information on page 29 and the sample above to solve the long division problems on this page. Use a calculator to check your answers.

1.
$$369) \overline{9745}$$

2.
$$298) \overline{6834}$$

3.
$$499) \overline{5673}$$

4.
$$567) \overline{6289}$$

5.
$$896) \overline{9561}$$

6.
$$299) \overline{9239}$$

7.
$$894) \overline{9835}$$

8.
$$221) \overline{8965}$$

Follow these steps to solve long division problems using estimation and a calculator.

1. Round the divisor to the nearest 1,000.

2. Round the dividend to the nearest 10,000 or 100,000.

3. Divide and estimate the quotient.

4. Find the actual answer by solving the long division on another sheet of paper.

5. Compare the actual answer and your estimate.

6. Check your answer by using a calculator to check your calculations. You should notice that all three answers—estimated, actual, and calculated—should be very close.

Directions: Use the information given above to solve these long division problems. Solve the problems by using estimation, the Division Code, and a calculator.

Estimation	Division Code	Calculator
1.	$4{,}234\overline{)91{,}329}$	
2.	$2{,}963\overline{)66{,}832}$	
3.	$2{,}119\overline{)89{,}371}$	
4.	$3{,}112\overline{)23{,}432}$	

Facts to Know

Averages

An *average* is found by adding all the numbers in a group together and dividing that total by the number of items in the group.

Sample

John had these grades on 5 spelling tests: 100, 78, 92, 86, and 94

1. Add all the scores that John received on his tests:

   $100 + 78 + 92 + 86 + 94 = 450$

2. Divide the total by the number of grades.

3. The average grade on the 5 tests is 90.

$$\begin{array}{r} \mathbf{x90} \\ 5\overline{)\,450} \\ -\,45\!\downarrow \\ \hline 0 \\ -\,0 \\ \hline 0 \end{array}$$

Sequences

A *sequence* is a set of numbers in which the numbers have an exact order and follow a rule.

Samples

2,500, 500, 100, 20 → Rule: Divide by 5.

4,096, 1,024, 256, 64, 16 → Rule: Divide by 4.

Functions

A *function* is a rule that converts the numbers in one set into another set of numbers. It must be applied the same way to each number in the set.

Study these examples:

n	f(n)	n	f(n)	n	f(n)
20	10	20	11	4	2
30	15	30	16	9	3
40	20	40	21	16	4
50	25	50	26	25	5
Rule: $f(n) = n \div 2$		Rule: $f(n) = (n \div 2) + 1$		Rule: $f(n) = \sqrt{n}$	

The f(n) is called the function of n. It is the number produced after the rule is applied to the first number.

- The rule of the first function was "divide by 2."

  Example: The number 20 divided by 2 is 10.

- The rule of the second function was "divide by 2 and add 1."

  Example: The number 20 divided by 2 is 10 and adding 1 makes 11.

- The rule of the third function was "square root" of the number.

  Example: The square root of 4 is 2.

Notice that each group of numbers with the same function obeys the rule.

An **average** for a set of numbers is calculated by adding all the numbers in the set together and dividing this sum by the total number of items in the set.

Melissa took 4 math tests and received the following grades: 88, 94, 100, and 98. What was her average grade?

1. Add all the grades.

2. Divide the total by the number of grades.

3. Melissa's average grade is 95.

```
  88          x95
  94        4) 380
 100         - 36↓
+ 98           20
————         - 20
 380           0
```

Directions: Use the information on page 32 and in the sample above to compute the averages in the problems below.

1. Bobby has 98 baseball cards. His brother Marco has 88. His friend Juan has 100 and Juan's cousins have 76 and 58 cards. What is the average number of baseball cards among the 5 boys?_____

2. Sarah has 100 stickers while her friend Emily has 65. Molly has 92 stickers while her sister Grace has 83. What is the average number of stickers among the 4 girls?_____

3. The 4 members of the Sanchez family had the following bowling scores: 228, 140, 184, and 120. What was the average bowling score for the Sanchez family?_____

4. Here is a list of the Milton High School basketball team's scores in 6 basketball games: 88, 72, 60, 85, 93, and 58. What is the average number of points per game?
_____

5. Harry took 8 math quizzes and received the following grades: 88, 100, 98, 94, 97, 83, 77, and 87. What is Harry's average quiz score?_____

6. Kendra baked 16 cookies. Suzy baked 24 cookies. Sara baked 34 cookies. Erica baked 30 cookies. What is the average number of cookies that these 4 girls baked?
_____

7. There are 5 puzzles in Ms. Chang's classroom. The puzzles have the following number of puzzle pieces: 200, 500, 1,200, 750, and 600. What is the average number of pieces for a puzzle in Ms. Chang's classroom?_____

8. Noriko has $15, Alexa has $22, Pedro has $18, and Kim has $30. What is the average amount of money for this group of friends?_____

A **sequence** is a set of numbers in which the numbers have an exact order and follow a rule.

Example: This sequence **88, 44, 22, 11** follows this rule: **divide by 2.**

Directions: Find the rule to these sequences and complete the unfinished sequences.

Sequence	**Rule**
1. 99, 33, 11	_____
2. 500, 250, 125, 62.5	_____
3. 500, 100, 20, 4	_____
4. 64, 16, 4, 1	_____
5. 64, 32, 16, 8, 4	_____
6. 81, 27, 9, 3, 1	_____
7. 625, 125, 25, 5, 1	_____
8. 1,296, 216, 36, 6, 1	_____
9. 32,768, 4,096, 512, _____, _____, _____	_____
10. 1,000,000, 100,000, 10,000, _____, _____, _____	_____
11. 248,832, 20,736, 1,728, _____, _____, _____	_____
12. 759,375, 50,625, 3,375, _____, _____, _____	_____
13. 531,441, 59,049, 6,561, _____, _____, _____	_____
14. 117,649, 16,807, 2,401, _____, _____, _____	_____

Study these functions:

n	f(n)		n	f(n)		n	f(n)
9	3		9	5		9	2
15	5		15	7		15	4
21	7		21	9		21	6
30	10		30	12		30	9
Rule: $f(n) = n \div 3$			**Rule:** $f(n) = (n \div 3) + 2$			**Rule:** $f(n) = (n \div 3) - 1$	

Remember, a rule applies to every number in the same function.

Directions: Use the information on page 32 and the samples above to help you solve these functions. The rule for each function is stated above the function.

1. Rule: $f(n) = n \div 4$

n	f(n)
16	_____
20	_____
28	_____
36	_____
40	_____
48	_____

2. Rule: $f(n) = (n \div 4) + 2$

n	f(n)
16	_____
20	_____
28	_____
36	_____
40	_____
48	_____

3. Rule: $f(n) = n \div 5$

n	f(n)
25	_____
35	_____
50	_____
70	_____
75	_____
100	_____

4. Rule: $f(n) = (n \div 5) - 3$

n	f(n)
25	_____
35	_____
50	_____
70	_____
75	_____
100	_____

5. Rule: $f(n) = n \div 10$

n	f(n)
80	_____
100	_____
150	_____
180	_____
220	_____
240	_____

6. Rule: $f(n) = (n \div 10) + 4$

n	f(n)
90	_____
120	_____
200	_____
250	_____
300	_____
360	_____

Find the rule and fill in the blanks.

7. Rule: $f(n) =$ _____

n	f(n)
100	13
160	15
220	_____
260	_____
300	_____
340	_____
420	_____
500	_____

8. Rule: $f(n) =$ _____

n	f(n)
100	11
150	13
225	_____
275	_____
325	_____
400	_____
475	_____
525	_____

•••• Solve Square Roots and Divide with Different Division Formats

Facts to Know

Square Roots

The *square root* of a number is another number that multiplied by itself will equal the first number.

The square root of 4 is 2 because 2 x 2 = 4.

This symbol $\sqrt{}$ is called the radical and indicates that you need to find the square root.

$$\sqrt{9} = 3 \qquad\qquad\qquad \sqrt{16} = 4$$

Different Division Formats

As you become more advanced in math, you will see division expressed in different ways:

Horizontal Format: This expression is written across rather than under the division frame.

$$21 \div 3 = 7 \qquad\qquad 100 \div 5 = 20$$

Fraction Bar: This expression is usually used in algebra. The dividend is written over the divisor like this:

$$\frac{6}{3} = 2 \qquad\qquad \frac{45}{5} = 9 \qquad\qquad \frac{100}{20} = 5$$

Decimals: A *decimal* is used in a number to represent a part of a whole number (or fraction) and to indicate where the digits in a number are located in terms of their place value.

$$7.25 = 7\,\frac{25}{100} = 7\frac{1}{4} \qquad\qquad 14.14 = 14\,\frac{14}{100} = 14\frac{7}{50}$$

When dividing with decimals, remember to write the decimal point in the correct place in the quotient. For whole-number divisors involving money, bring the decimal and the dollar sign straight up. See the examples below.

$$\begin{array}{r} \$1.65 \\ \hline 5\,)\,\$8.25 \end{array} \qquad\qquad\qquad \begin{array}{r} \$\ 28.10 \\ \hline 4\,)\,\$112.40 \end{array}$$

Percents: A *percent* is a number that represents a fraction or part of a hundred (or any number).

Sample

Michael wanted to buy a special set of baseball cards to add to his collection. He saved his money and bought 8 out of 15 cards available. What percentage of cards has Michael purchased so far?

1. Divide the number of cards that Michael has (8) by the total number of cards available (15).
2. Because 8 is not divisible by 15, add a decimal and two zeros as placeholders.
3. The final answer is 0.53 or 53% because $0.53 = \frac{53}{100} = 53\%$.

$$\begin{array}{r} 0.53 \\ 15\,)\,\overline{8.00} \\ -7\,5\downarrow \\ \hline 50 \\ -45 \\ \hline 5 \end{array}$$

You can convert a decimal into a percent and a percent into a decimal equivalent. Numbers written in percent form or with decimals represent fractions or parts of a whole number.

The **square root** of a number is another number that multiplied by itself will equal the first number.

The square root of 9 is 3 because 3 x 3 = 9.

This radical symbol $\sqrt{}$ indicates that you need to find the square root.

$$\sqrt{25} = 5 \qquad\qquad \sqrt{36} = 6$$

Directions: Use the information on page 36 and the samples above to help solve these problems. Use a calculator to help you check the answers on the more difficult problems.

1. $\sqrt{4}$ = _____

2. $\sqrt{16}$ = _____

3. $\sqrt{49}$ = _____

4. $\sqrt{81}$ = _____

5. $\sqrt{100}$ = _____

6. $\sqrt{64}$ = _____

7. $\sqrt{121}$ = _____

8. $\sqrt{144}$ = _____

9. $\sqrt{169}$ = _____

10. $\sqrt{225}$ = _____

11. $\sqrt{196}$ = _____

12. $\sqrt{400}$ = _____

13. $\sqrt{900}$ = _____

14. $\sqrt{4900}$ = _____

15. $\sqrt{6400}$ = _____

16. $\sqrt{1600}$ = _____

17. $\sqrt{490,000}$ = _____

18. $\sqrt{640,000}$ = _____

19. $\sqrt{160,000}$ = _____

20. $\sqrt{810,000}$ = _____

21. $\sqrt{250,000}$ = _____

22. $\sqrt{90,000}$ = _____

23. $\sqrt{360,000}$ = _____

24. $\sqrt{10,000}$ = _____

25. $\sqrt{9,000,000}$ = _____

26. $\sqrt{81,000,000}$ = _____

27. $\sqrt{25,000,000}$ = _____

28. $\sqrt{36,000,000}$ = _____

29. $\sqrt{49,000,000}$ = _____

30. $\sqrt{64,000,000}$ = _____

Horizontal Format: This expression is written across.

$$24 \div 6 = 4 \qquad\qquad 144 \div 12 = 12$$

Fraction Bar: The dividend is written over the divisor.

$$\frac{9}{3} = 3 \qquad \frac{81}{9} = 9 \qquad \frac{300}{30} = 10 \qquad \frac{1,000}{100} = 10$$

Directions: Study the information on page 36 and the samples above to solve the problems below.

1. $28 \div 7 =$

2. $100 \div 10 =$

3. $99 \div 9 =$

4. $49 \div 7 =$

5. $300 \div 30 =$

6. $77 \div 7 =$

7. $200 \div 5 =$

8. $250 \div 50 =$

9. $400 \div 40 =$

10. $279 \div 9 =$

11. $363 \div 3 =$

12. $540 \div 9 =$

13. $3330 \div 9 =$

14. $213 \div 3 =$

15. $111 \div 3 =$

16. $\dfrac{484}{4} =$

17. $\dfrac{124}{4} =$

18. $\dfrac{924}{4} =$

19. $\dfrac{230}{10} =$

20. $\dfrac{490}{10} =$

21. $\dfrac{860}{10} =$

22. $\dfrac{275}{25} =$

23. $\dfrac{525}{25} =$

24. $\dfrac{925}{25} =$

25. $\dfrac{1450}{50} =$

26. $\dfrac{2900}{50} =$

27. $\dfrac{4850}{50} =$

28. $\dfrac{4590}{90} =$

29. $\dfrac{2340}{90} =$

30. $\dfrac{9360}{90} =$

Practice ・・・・・ **Dividing with Decimals and Money**

When solving long division problems that involve decimals, keep the following in mind:

- Place the decimal (and dollar sign when money is involved) in the quotient.

- Use the Division Code to solve each problem.

- Numbers with decimals are another way of representing a part of a whole (or a fraction of a whole).

Directions: Use the information on page 36 and in the chart above to solve the division problems below. Remember to bring the decimal point and dollar sign straight up.

1. $8)\overline{16.80}$

2. $12)\overline{14.88}$

3. $5)\overline{62.25}$

4. $4)\overline{164.4}$

5. $5)\overline{8624.5}$

6. $4)\overline{4253}$

7. $7)\overline{4526.03}$

8. $8)\overline{1257.30}$

9. $12)\overline{\$56.76}$

10. $12)\overline{\$4234.56}$

11. $17)\overline{\$3489.76}$

12. $34)\overline{\$5189.08}$

When solving for percentages, remember the following:

• Percents can be represented as fractions with a denominator of 100.

Examples: $35\% = \dfrac{35}{100}$ $12\% = \dfrac{12}{100}$

• Fractions can be converted to decimals by dividing the numerator by the denominator. Convert decimals to percents by moving the decimal point two places to the right and adding a percent sign (%). (**Note:** If the decimal point is already at the end of number, it is not necessary to place it. Just add a % sign.)

Examples: $\dfrac{3}{5} = .60 = 60\%$ $\dfrac{7}{10} = .70 = 70\%$
$5\overline{)3.00}$ $10\overline{)7.00}$

Directions: Use the information on page 36 and the information above to solve the percent problems below. For some of the problems, a fraction is given that has to be converted to a percentage. In other problems a percentage is given that has to be converted to a fraction. There are also some challenging word problems at the bottom of this page that involve percents.

1. $56\% =$

2. $\dfrac{4}{5} =$

3. $\dfrac{6}{7} =$

4. $38\% =$

5. $\dfrac{9}{400} =$

6. $57\% =$

7. $28\% =$

8. $\dfrac{5}{9} =$

9. $67\% =$

10. $\dfrac{12}{56} =$

11. $88\% =$

12. $\dfrac{3}{8} =$

13. $\dfrac{36}{96} =$

14. $52\% =$

15. $\dfrac{33}{78} =$

16. $49\% =$

17. The children in Mrs. Smith's first-grade class brought their stuffed animals to class for show and tell. There are 17 children in her class, and 14 remembered to bring their stuffed animals to class. What percentage of children brought their stuffed animals to class? _____

18. Robin and her sister Molly collected dolls. They wanted to collect a set of special dolls in the Lily Rose series. There are 25 dolls in the series. Robin and Molly had 17 dolls. What percentage of the dolls in the series did the sisters have? _____

19. On his most recent math test, Jimmy solved 27 out of 30 problems. What is his grade (or percentage) for this test? _____

20. The Chen family ordered two large pizzas. If 13 of the 16 pieces were eaten, what percentage of the pieces were eaten? _____

Dr. Dooley D. Vision is known as The Great Divider. He just loves to divide things. It's his favorite job. He does need a little help, however. Solve the division problems below to make sure he gets the right answers.

1. Dr. Dooley D. Vision has a collection of 144 used baseballs which he is going to divide evenly among his 6 grandchildren. How many baseballs will each of the 6 grandchildren receive? _____

2. Dr. Dooley has collected quarters for years. He has 4,575 quarters which he intends to divide evenly among a class of 25 smart fifth graders. How many quarters will each fifth grader receive? _____

3. The Great Divider has acquired a pile of 1,863 packs of gum which he intends to divide evenly among 9 children living on his street. How many packs of gum will each child receive? _____

4. Dr. D. Vision was hired by a large family of squirrels to help them split a hoard of 5,380 nuts among the 20 members of the squirrel family. How many nuts did each squirrel get? _____

5. The good doctor was asked to divide a special collection of 1,350 baseball cards among 50 deserving fourth graders. How many cards did each child receive? _____

6. Doctor Dooley was hired to split a gigantic mound of 45,360 Sweet 'n Sour Suckers among 90 sixth graders at the Okie Dokie Elementary School. How many suckers did each sixth grader get? _____

7. Dr. Dooley D. Vision had an opportunity to divide 15,575 pennies among a troop of 25 Girl Scouts. How many pennies did each Girl Scout receive? _____

8. Dooley was honored to distribute 16,485 sunflower seeds among a family of 21 chipmunks. How many seeds did each chipmunk receive? _____

9. Dr. D. Vision was asked to divide equally 228 fish into 6 fish tanks. How many fish will there be in each tank? _____

10. The doctor needs to equally divide 11,410 marbles among 10 children. How many marbles will each child receive? _____

Buggsy Beetlehead is the world's most famous bug collector. His farm is overflowing with beetles, caterpillars, house flies, horse flies, bottle flies, bedbugs, toad bugs, ambush bugs, and fleas of every description. It has gotten a little overcrowded. Help Buggsy rearrange his collection into new living quarters.

1. Buggsy's huge collection of 6,998 toad bugs needs to be divided among 23 cages.

    How many toad bugs will be in each cage? _____

    How many toad bugs will be left over? _____

2. Buggsy Beetlehead's hoard of 3,498 house flies needs to be housed in 21 fly flats.

    How many flies will be in each flat? _____

    How many flies will be left over? _____

3. The Great Collector's stockpile of 16,498 bottle flies is to be divided into 29 cottages.

    How many bottle flies will be in each cottage? _____

    How many bottle flies will be left over? _____

4. Buggsy is batty over bedbugs. He has accumulated 20,302 of them which he intends to divide among 39 beds.

    How many bedbugs will be in each bed? _____

    How many bedbugs will be left over? _____

5. The Beetlehead Farm boasts of having 69,459 stag beetles which will be divided among 31 condos.

    How many stag beetles will live in each condo? _____

    How many stag beetles will be left over? _____

6. The World's Greatest Collector is very proud of his flea farm which has 15,692 fleas. He intends to divide them among 27 tents.

    How many fleas will be in each tent? _____

    How many fleas will be left over? _____

7. Mr. Beetlehead's assortment of 53,439 ambush bugs will be divided among 42 apartments.

    How many ambush bugs will be living in each apartment? _____

    How many ambush bugs will be left over? _____

8. Buggsy has 365,893 horse flies which he intends to house in 18 stables.

    How many horse flies will live in each stable? _____

    How many horse flies will be left over? _____

•••••••••• **Multiple Order of Operations**

Directions: Using multiplication and division, solve the problems below. Remember, you can only use multiplication and division. The first one is done for you as an example.

1.	1 x 9 x 8 ÷ 12 = 6						
2.	15	15	5	9	3	=	15
3.	56	4	7	2		=	4
4.	156	4	2	2		=	156
5.	635	6	10	3		=	127
6.	77	11	8	14		=	4
7.	25	60	10	15		=	10
8.	72	8	9	4	6	=	54
9.	145	5	4	2		=	232
10.	8460	10	94	2		=	18

Directions: For each problem unscramble the dividend and/or the divisor to find the given quotient. The first one is done for you as an example.

1.	$414 \div 12 = 12 \longrightarrow$	$144 \div 12 = 12$
2.	$661 \div 41 = 44 \longrightarrow$	
3.	$913 \div 92 = 11 \longrightarrow$	
4.	$753 \div 51 = 25 \longrightarrow$	
5.	$594 \div 15 = 63 \longrightarrow$	
6.	$2765 \div 64 = 56 \longrightarrow$	
7.	$0390 \div 026 = 15 \longrightarrow$	
8.	$2179 \div 91 = 19 \longrightarrow$	
9.	$9849 \div 17 = 69 \longrightarrow$	
10.	$5598 \div 939 = 15 \longrightarrow$	

12 Technology • • • **Working with Fractions and Percents**

Students will be collecting data, analyzing that data, and using it to create a bar graph to reinforce their understanding of fractions and percentages. They should be familiar with spreadsheet software and how to make graphs on them.

Materials

- computer
- calculator
- Class Survey Data Sheet (page 46)
- spreadsheet program such as *Microsoft Excel* ®

Internet Link

http://yn.la.ca.us/cec/cecmath/math-elem.html

Directions

1. Take a survey of the information needed to complete the data sheet on page 46. Count the number of people in your class who fit each characteristic. Write the total for each part of the survey. Keep in mind that each number represents a percentage or fraction of the class population which fits this characteristic.

2. Use a calculator to convert each fraction into a percentage. Remember that the total number of people who fit each characteristic is the numerator and the total number of students in the class is the denominator.

3. Open a new document in the spreadsheet software and type each characteristic in a separate cell in the first column.

4. In the next column, type in the percentage of students who fit each characteristic.

5. Convert your information into a column graph by selecting the graphing function found on most spreadsheet programs. Give a title to your survey and label the x-axis and y-axis.

6. Print out your survey and write a short summary about the results and conclusions that you have gathered about your classmates.

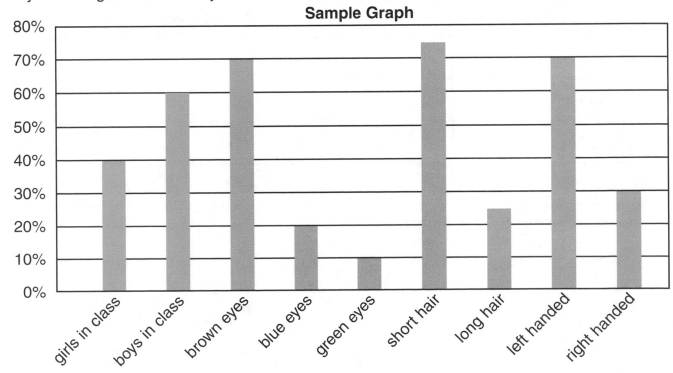

Sample Graph

••• Working with Fractions and Percents

Class Survey Data Sheet

Characteristics	Number of Students	Fraction	Percent
1. number of boys			
2. number of girls			
3. brown eyes			
4. blue eyes			
5. green eyes			
6. wears sneakers			
7. doesn't wear sneakers			
8. blonde hair			
9. red hair			
10. brown hair			
11. black hair			
12. left handed			
13. right handed			
14. long hair			
15. short hair			

Survey Summary and Conclusions

_____

_____

_____

_____

Page 6

1. 11 R1
2. 16 R4
3. 13
4. 11 R1
5. 28 R2
6. 24 R3
7. 9
8. 34
9. 13
10. 10 R6
11. 11 R1
12. 14 R1
13. 16 R1
14. 18 R2
15. 11 R2
16. 16 R3
17. 23
18. 6 R4
19. 8 R4
20. 9 R2
21. 10
22. 5
23. 12 R2
24. 21 R3
25. 23 R1

Page 7

1. 91
2. 71 R1
3. 62
4. 62 R3
5. 53 R1
6. 52
7. 54 R1
8. 79 R6
9. 62 R5
10. 75 R3
11. 99 R2
12. 57

Page 8

1. 612 R1
2. 691 R1
3. 374 R4
4. 417 R3
5. 887 R4
6. 489 R1
7. 1125 R4
8. 1455 R1
9. 1090 R3

Page 10

1. 381
2. 93
3. 124
4. 41
5. 143
6. 135
7. 224
8. 88
9. 174
10. 225
11. 2967
12. 1420
13. 3956
14. 1046
15. 3269
16. 1184

Page 11

1. 91
2. 54
3. 85
4. 79
5. 62
6. 56
7. 45
8. 107
9. 31
10. 67
11. 743
12. 577
13. 1091
14. 561
15. 369
16. 1404

Page 12

1. 238
2. 704
3. 999
4. 1604
5. 2312
6. 479
7. 212
8. 1741
9. 703
10. 1714
11. 1981
12. 191

Page 14

1. 37
2. 57
3. 66
4. 456
5. 743
6. 76
7. 67
8. 54
9. 77
10. 23
11. 998
12. 447
13. 168
14. 345
15. 678

Page 15

1. 23
2. 22
3. 21
4. 32 R6
5. 12 R9
6. 34 R7
7. 42 R9
8. 47 R16
9. 24 R9
10. 150
11. 211
12. 443
13. 232
14. 321
15. 233
16. 161 R7

Page 16

1. 173
2. 903
3. 69
4. 200
5. 150
6. 486
7. 51
8. 134
9. 83
10. 81
11. 75
12. 62

Page 18

1. 21 R17
2. 31 R14
3. 32 R12
4. 31 R10
5. 15 R2
6. 11 R2
7. 42 R5
8. 21 R22
9. 23 R13
10. 13 R25
11. 22 R6
12. 32 R17

Page 19

1. 23 R10
2. 26 R26
3. 21 R9
4. 11 R36
5. 34 R16
6. 23 R13
7. 24 R12
8. 23 R15
9. 22 R13
10. 31 R10
11. 15 R36
12. 22 R9
13. 21 R22
14. 23 R14
15. 34 R15
16. 33 R14

Page 20

1. 185 R14
2. 215 R21
3. 244 R29
4. 224 R3
5. 358 R13
6. 182 R27
7. 213 R10
8. 256 R5
9. 251 R13

Page 22

1. 90 R2
2. 203 R2
3. 1002 R1
4. 1003 R4
5. 800 R3
6. 700 R6
7. 10 R15
8. 103 R11
9. 200 R4
10. 202 R22
11. 305 R5
12. 204 R5

Page 23

1. 205 R12
2. 209 R25
3. 105 R19
4. 209 R24
5. 309 R11
6. 109 R4
7. 207 R20
8. 209
9. 308 R9

Page 24

10. 209 R13
11. 208 R28
12. 297 R13

Page 24

1. 205 R21
2. 100 R22
3. 204 R35
4. 208 R31
5. 209 R33
6. 209 R22
7. 309 R15
8. 109 R65
9. 209 R18
10. 309 R16
11. 209 R34
12. 100 R35

Page 26

	Actual	Estimate
1.	19 R9	20
2.	21 R22	20
3.	22 R9	20
4.	34 R21	30
5.	20 R21	20
6.	222 R21	200

Page 27

1. 19 R9
2. 22 R29
3. 36 R9
4. 31 R14
5. 23 R25
6. 155 R11

Page 28

1. 304 R11
2. 210 R4
3. 310 R5
4. 103 R60
5. 84
6. 176 R24
7. 110 R54
8. 229 R40
9. 217 R2
10. 1141 R18
11. 201 R55
12. 997 R4

Page 30

1. 26 R151
2. 22 R278
3. 11 R184
4. 11 R52
5. 10 R601
6. 30 R269
7. 11 R1
8. 40 R125

Page 31

Estimation	Division Code	Calculator
1. 22.5	21 R2415	21.57
2. 23	22 R1646	22.55
3. 45	42 R373	42.17
4. 7	7 R1648	7.53

Page 33

1. 84 cards
2. 85 stickers
3. 168 points
4. 76 points
5. 90.5
6. 26 cookies
7. 650 pieces
8. $21.25

Page 34

1. divide by 3
2. divide by 2
3. divide by 5
4. divide by 4
5. divide by 2
6. divide by 3
7. divide by 5
8. divide by 6
9. 64, 8, 1
   divide by 8
10. 1,000, 100, 10
    divide by 10
11. 144, 12, 1
    divide by 12
12. 225, 15, 1
    divide by 15
13. 729, 81, 9
    divide by 9
14. 343, 49, 7
    divide by 7

Page 35

1. 4, 5, 7, 9, 10, 12
2. 6, 7, 9, 11, 12, 14
3. 5, 7, 10, 14, 15, 20
4. 2, 4, 7, 11, 12, 17
5. 8, 10, 15, 18, 22, 24
6. 13, 16, 24, 29, 34, 40
7. (n ÷ 20) + 8
   13, 15, 17, 21, 25
8. (n ÷ 25) + 7
   11, 13, 16, 19, 21

Page 37

1. 2
2. 4

3. 7
4. 9
5. 10
6. 8
7. 11
8. 12
9. 13
10. 15
11. 14
12. 20
13. 30
14. 70
15. 80
16. 40
17. 700
18. 800
19. 400
20. 900
21. 500
22. 300
23. 600
24. 100
25. 3,000
26. 9,000
27. 5,000
28. 6,000
29. 7,000
30. 8,000

Page 38

1. 4
2. 10
3. 11
4. 7
5. 10
6. 11
7. 40
8. 5
9. 10
10. 31
11. 121
12. 60
13. 370
14. 71
15. 37
16. 121
17. 31
18. 231
19. 23
20. 49
21. 86
22. 11
23. 21
24. 37
25. 29

26. 58
27. 97
28. 51
29. 26
30. 104

Page 39

1. 2.1
2. 1.24
3. 12.45
4. 41.1
5. 1724.9
6. 1063.25
7. 646.57
8. 157.16
9. $4.73
10. $352.88
11. $205.28
12. $152.88

Page 40

1. 56/100 = 14/25
2. 80%
3. 86%
4. 38/100 = 19/50
5. 2.25%
6. 57/100
7. 28/100 = 7/25
8. 55.5%
9. 67/100
10. 21%
11. 88/100 = 22/25
12. 37.5%
13. 37.5%
14. 52/100 = 13/25
15. 42%
16. 49/100
17. 82%
18. 68%
19. 90%
20. 81%

Page 41

1. 24 baseballs
2. 183 quarters
3. 207 packs of gum
4. 269 nuts
5. 27 cards
6. 504 suckers
7. 623 pennies
8. 785 seeds
9. 38 fish per tank
10. 1141 marbles per child

Page 42

1. 304 bugs
   6 bugs
2. 166 flies
   12 flies
3. 568 bottle flies
   26 bottle flies
4. 520 bedbugs
   22 bedbugs
5. 2,240 beetles
   19 beetles
6. 581 fleas
   5 fleas
7. 1,272 bugs
   15 bugs
8. 20,327 horse flies
   7 horse flies

Page 43

1. 1 x 9 x 8 ÷ 12 = 6
2. 15 x 15 ÷ 5 ÷ 9 x 3 = 15
3. 56 ÷ 4 ÷ 7 x 2 = 4
4. 156 ÷ 4 x 2 x 2 = 156
5. 635 x 6 ÷ 10 ÷ 3 = 127
6. 77 ÷ 11 x 8 ÷ 14 = 4
7. 25 x 60 ÷ 10 ÷ 15 = 10
8. 72 ÷ 8 x 9 x 4 ÷ 6 = 54
9. 145 ÷ 5 x 4 x 2 = 232
10. 8460 ÷ 10 ÷ 94 x 2 = 18

Page 44

1. 144 ÷ 12 = 12
2. 616 ÷ 14 = 44
3. 319 ÷ 29 = 11
4. 375 ÷ 15 = 25
5. 945 ÷ 15 = 63
6. 2576 ÷ 46 = 56
7. 3900 ÷ 260 = 15
8. 1729 ÷ 91 = 19
9. 4899 ÷ 71 = 69
10. 5985 ÷ 399 = 15